DERBYSHIRE PRIVIES

DERBYSHIRE PRIVIES

by

DAVID BELL

COUNTRYSIDE BOOKS

NEWBURY · BERKSHIRE

First published 1998
© David Bell 1998

COUNTRYSIDE BOOKS
3 Catherine Road
Newbury, Berkshire

ISBN 1 85306 510 2

Produced through MRM Associates Ltd., Reading
Typeset by Techniset Typesetters, Merseyside
Printed by Woolnough Bookbinding Ltd., Irthlingborough

CONTENTS

For Jack Bell (1908–1996)

and all those who are

'Derbyshire born and Derbyshire bred
Strong in the arm and quick in the head.'

FOREWORD

Much of the information in this book came in letters and telephone calls from Derbyshire residents, in response to my broadcasts on Radio Derby and my letters in local newspapers. People from Swadlincote to Chesterfield, from Shardlow to Whaley Bridge, sent me their reminiscences. Some were humorous, some just grateful that the earth closet had been replaced by the flushing loo, others frankly nostalgic for the good old days. Many invited me to their cottage, their farm, or on a couple of occasions their stately home, to see the privy at the bottom of their garden. Whether speaking to members of Bakewell Historical Society or Stanton-by-Dale WI, I found that most Derbyshire people understood my fascination with the subject, though from time to time I did encounter puzzled folk who asked 'But why privies?'

One answer must be that the story of the privy is part of our local heritage, just as vital a part of Derbyshire's history as all those kings and battles. Whether it is called a privy, a closet, a midden, a lavatory, a jakes, a jericho, a necessarium or a close stool, it is a place we all need to visit on a regular basis. It is the most levelling of institutions, as applicable to miners and road-sweepers as to Prime Ministers and Archbishops. As Montaigne put it, 'Both Kings and philosophers obey nature and go to stool, and so do ladies.'

Advice given to me by a wonderful old character from Bolsover was that whenever anyone – a teacher, a preacher, a gaffer or a bureaucrat – was giving him a hard time, he just imagined them sitting on their privy! 'It works every time, me duck,' I was assured. I therefore pass the advice on to you as the perfect solution for when you are being subjected to verbal intimidation from anyone who is full of their own self-importance.

Some VIPs have tried to hide the fact of their natural human needs. One Egyptian Pharaoh, wishing to appear divine, used to rise early in the morning before anyone else was awake. He

The author looking pleased with his find at Kennel Cottages, Calke.

would go out into the desert to obey both the minor and major calls of nature, so that during the daytime he might appear to his subjects to be immune from such mortal necessities.

Others had been wiser. When Antigonus was called the 'Son of Apollo' by a flattering Roman poet, he replied that the man who emptied his close stool knew him better. Somerset Maugham wrote that he wished that his Lordship at the Old Bailey had, besides his bunch of flowers, a packet of toilet paper to remind him that he was a man like any other. I know my friend from Bolsover would concur.

The privy has played its part in royal history too. Charles of Spain was born in one, George II and another 'King', Elvis Presley, each died in one. James I of Scotland and Edmund Ironside were both murdered in a privy. There is a legend that Richard III plotted the murder of his nephews while sitting on a jakes, though members of the Richard III society would certainly not accept that.

A democratic place indeed.

One early reference to building a simple privy occurs in Deuteronomy, the fifth book of the Bible, where Moses tells his people, 'Thou shall have a place also without the camp, whither thou shall go forth abroad: And thou shall have a paddle upon thy weapon; and it shall be, when thou wilt ease thyself abroad, thou shalt dig therewith, and shalt turn back and cover that which cometh from thee.'

This is an excellent description of a basic privy, and not dissimilar from privies constructed by builders of our own day when first moving onto a building site. I spoke to one man who had been a carpenter on Derbyshire building sites for many decades. His first job was always to dig a deep hole for the men to use as a latrine. He then built a structure consisting of a strong horizontal wooden beam for the men to sit on, completing his work by putting up four walls and – if they were lucky – a roof. This simple structure could be moved to another location on the site if the building work took longer than the hole took to fill!

I suppose that, in this introduction, I really ought to define the word privy. According to the *Shorter Oxford Dictionary*, a privy is a lavatory, especially an outside one or one without plumbing. So I have, in the main, used the word to mean an outside lavatory where the sewage is either collected in a pit below the privy, or in a bucket. However, I have also investigated the indoor privy of castle life, often called a garderobe, and the much later outdoor WC, which was a flushing privy usually connected to the sewerage system.

A final word of thanks to my family who put up with my enthusiastic cries of 'Guess what. I've found a three-holer!' whenever I returned from an expedition to some remote part of northern Derbyshire. They managed to keep their faces straight, though they may well have secretly agreed with those pals who made the most of the opportunity to comment that, 'You always were round the bend, David!' or 'You are a little potty'. One wittier friend came up with, 'Yes, you always did like sticking your nose into other people's . . .'

DAVID BELL

[1]

A QUICK GALLOP THROUGH HISTORY

The very first latrine was simply a hole in the ground, used once, then covered over and abandoned. This procedure, described in the Old Testament, suited a nomadic existence but in a settled community it made more sense for the hole in the ground to become a large pit, capable of being used over a period of time. Provide a seat of some kind, and walls to screen the user from the public gaze, and what you now have is a privy – literally, a private place.

Early Derbyshire privies had an ashpit, since it was found that adding ash – or sand – to the waste had the effect of covering it

Rachel Froggett wonders why there's a secret way into the back of this privy at Thorpe.

and absorbing the moisture. Often other waste from kitchens was thrown in with the privy dung, as the simplest means of disposal. It was many centuries before the ashpits were capped over, and a container of some kind placed under the privy. The only snag with this improvement was that where an ashpit needed digging out once or twice a year, the privy bucket needed emptying once a week! The preferred method of disposal of the privy waste was to empty it into a passing river, which took it away out of sight and out of mind. (And, just as important, out of smelling range.) If it became a nuisance downstream, that was someone else's problem. A better solution to the disposal problem was to store the waste for a year or so, then use it as fertiliser on the land.

At first, buckets were removed from the privy by lifting the seat up, but a later sophistication had a small door built into the back of the privy. This enabled the bucket to be removed more discreetly, preferably while the privy was not in use. In

A one-holer, complete with wide bucket, at Basset Barn Farm, Dale Abbey.

the towns and larger villages of Derbyshire, the local authority sent round workmen called nightsoil men, with a cart. The contents of the privy buckets were tipped into the cart and taken away. However, farms and isolated cottages did not get this valuable service; there the contents of the privy continued to be taken away and buried by the individual householder.

Inside the house or cottage, a container was often kept under the bed for use during the night, its contents being disposed of into the privy next morning. Many of the these containers – or chamber pots – were beautifully decorated, usually on the outside, but by about 1800, they were being manufactured with pictures or words on the inside. One popular design contained a picture of a large eye, and the words: 'Use me well and keep me clean, and I'll not tell what I have seen.' Another design popular in England contained a picture of Napoleon Bonaparte. It was possible for the owner of this pot to relieve himself and pass a comment on an enemy at the same time! Later, portraits of other unpopular characters were used.

In towns, disposal of the contents of the chamber pot was something of a problem, and the solution more casual. An upper floor window would open, and the contents would be thrown out into the street. Thoughtful people would cry out 'Gardy loo!' to give any unfortunate passers-by time to duck out of the way, though the cry was often too late. Having been hurled out of the window, the waste would lie in the middle of the road, until rain washed it further down the street.

In castles and manor houses, the indoor privy was known as a garderobe. Originally, the word meant a chamber where clothes were stored, but this room often had a small privy chamber attached, and over time the word garderobe became used for the privy itself. Since the word literally means a 'wardrobe', we might be tempted to smile at the medieval use of a euphemism, but we are no different today when we talk of needing to use the cloakroom. Most of the words used to denote a latrine are euphemisms. A privy means a private place, a toilet and a lavatory

This garderobe at Haddon Hall had a locking lid. The key to the executive loo is an older idea than you think!

The entry that led to a large communal latrine at Wingfield Manor, near Alfreton.

These gutters at Haddon Hall channelled rainwater into the chamber below the garderobes.

both denote a place for washing.

The garderobe was usually built into the thickness of a castle wall, so that the waste would drop into a channel within the wall, and then out at the wall's base. Where that was not possible, the garderobe protruded out of the wall in a corbel. Here waste simply dropped outside the castle walls onto the ground, or preferably into the moat. Some castles had an ingenious arrangement, whereby rainwater was channelled along gutters into the chamber below the garderobe to wash the waste out. In some large houses, the garderobe was situated over a chamber where the privy dung accumulated for six months at a time, until it was time for workmen to enter the place and shovel out the unpleasant waste.

Not all castles had garderobes. Some, like Bolsover Castle, had a close stool – a chamber pot built into a box or a seat – inside the privy. As with the cottage bucket closet, this had the

16

Each room of the 'Little Castle' at Bolsover Castle had a small chamber that once housed a stool closet.

disadvantage that someone had to empty the contents at regular intervals, taking the full containers quickly but extremely carefully down the servants' staircase!

One of the great names in the development of the privy is that of Sir John Harington. Harington was a genuinely original pioneer, centuries ahead of his time. Born in the West Country in 1561, he was the godson of Queen Elizabeth I. He was a writer of satires, a translator of Italian plays and poems, and above all – from our perspective – an inventor. Queen Elizabeth had mixed feelings about John Harington; she referred to him affectionately as 'that witty fellow, my godson' but also banished him from court on two occasions when his wit was too saucy for her taste.

During one of his banishments, Harington designed the first English water closet and had it made by a local craftsman, who is known only by his initials: T.C. Sir John named his invention The Mighty Ajax. This was a pun on the Elizabethan term for a privy: a jakes. The first Ajax – there were only ever two – was installed at Sir John's home near Bath in 1589.

Sir John described his invention in a book, *The Metamorphosis of Ajax*. He listed the materials needed to construct and install his flushing privy, calculating the total cost as 30s 6d. The book was virtually a do-it-yourself instruction manual. He included diagrams to show how the Ajax worked. When a handle in the seat was pulled, a valve released water from a cistern, which cascaded down the walls of the bowl, washing them thoroughly and flushing away the contents.

A second Ajax was built at Richmond Palace for the personal use of the Queen and her ladies. It is perhaps not surprising that Queen Elizabeth I should command her godson's invention to be installed there, since she was known to have an eccentric regard for hygiene. Her unusual devotion to cleanliness was notorious in court circles; she was even reputed to take a bath once a month 'whether she needed it or not!'

The mighty Ajax now had royal approval; what is more, *The*

Metamorphosis of Ajax became the very first privy book, a copy permanently on display in the Queen's privy chamber.

Although the first English flushing water closet was invented during the reign of Elizabeth I, the idea did not find many supporters. It was not until the 18th and 19th centuries that inventors like Alexander Cummings, Joseph Bramah and Thomas Crapper made the flushing loo a popular contraption.

Thomas Crapper is one of that renowned group of people whose name has created a new word in the language. Other common words coined from surnames include the hoover, the sandwich, diesel, wellingtons and those unforgettable bloomers. It has to be admitted that only part of Crapper's name made it into the vernacular but, like hoover, it can be a verb or a noun!

Thomas Crapper was born in Yorkshire in 1837, the same year that Queen Victoria came to the throne. When he was only eleven years of age, he walked to London in search of work, finding it in the employ of a master plumber. Thirteen years later, Thomas Crapper set up in business for himself as a sanitary engineer in Chelsea. He had picked a good time to do so, as London was beginning the building of over 80 miles of sewers.

One problem at that time was that a lavatory chain would release water until the puller let go, and many people tied down the chain to ensure a continuous flow of water into the lavatory pan. Very hygienic, but extremely wasteful! To solve this problem, Thomas Crapper invented what he called the Water Waste Preventer.

Inside the cistern of his WWP was a chamber. The action of the chain being pulled lifted a plate in the bottom of this chamber and forced water into the pipe that led to the lavatory bowl below. This siphoned all the rest of the water in the cistern into the chamber and down the pipe to the lavatory. There was now no point in members of the public tying the chain down; the modern pull-and-release action of chain technique had been born.

Thomas Crapper opened showrooms in King's Road, Chelsea.

SELF-ACTING CINDER SIFTER.

Amongst the many advantages of this novel and ingenious invention the most noticeable is the almost entire

ABSENCE OF TROUBLE AND DIRT.

The arrangement of Sifters being self-acting, it is merely necessary to empty the cinders into the hopper, and as they descend they are entirely separated, the ashes passing into the top drawer and the cinders into the lower one.

45/- each.

The cinder sifter separated ash to be used in an earth closet.

In Crapper & Co's workshop, he had a test panel of five toilets, served by a 200 gallon water tank on the roof. It was obviously not enough for water to come down the pipe; it had to do an efficient job of removing the contents of the lavatory bowl. One intriguing problem was what to use for the simulated contents of the pan. Crapper and his colleagues eventually decided on a mixture of plumber's grease (known as 'smudge'),

The ash was placed in the hopper and a measured amount was released when the handle was pulled.

Underneath was a pail (it held 20 'charges') or a tank on wheels. The tank could accommodate 44 'charges'.

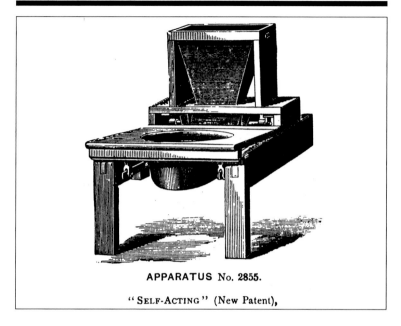

APPARATUS No. 2855.

" SELF-ACTING " (New Patent),

There was a version that worked automatically when the user stood up!

sponges, apples, cotton waste and 'air vessels'. The latter were paper bags containing air. It was recorded in 1884 that one flush shifted ten apples, a sponge, three air vessels, smudge smeared over the pan, and four pieces of paper stuck to the smudge. On another occasion, an over-enthusiastic apprentice threw his cap after this mixture, and that too was successfully flushed away!

During World War I, American servicemen based in Britain noticed the name Thomas Crapper on toilets, and began to say 'I'm off to the Crapper!' From there, it mutated to 'I'm going for a crap'. After the war, they took the word crap – initially as a euphemism for faeces and later as a general word for rubbish or nonsense – back to the USA. The word came back to Britain along with many other American vernacular terms during the 1920s.

Of course no system works for ever, without maintenance. Many a chain-puller has found that with an old WC, the simple pull-and-release technique isn't enough. Individual WCs each demand an individual approach. 'Ours needs two quick pulls and then a slow one' is the sort of advice given to guests attempting to flush these older lavatories.

Despite the invention of the WC, many people remained faithful to the traditional privy, and the inventive Victorians put their mind to their needs too. One wonderful creation was a self-acting cinder sifter that would sort out ash from cinders. The ash could then be used in an earth closet, where the user could pull a lever when he had used the privy. This released a quantity of ash, which fell into the privy bucket to cover the contents. For another invention, it was not even necessary to pull a lever or a chain! This was an automatic earth closet where, when the user had finished and stood up, the ash would automatically descend onto the waste. Yet another patent was for a self-acting water closet; this had water flushing automatically when the user stood up after using the WC.

Stories of a Victorian loo that automatically played the National Anthem when the would-be-user sat on the toilet seat are completely apocryphal, but they would certainly prove a frustrating device. The man would sit, the National Anthem would play. If he were patriotic, the poor man would rise to his feet until the tune was finished. Then he would sit again, the National Anthem would play ... ad infinitum. He could never complete what he had come for!

The first WC to be installed in a train, in this country, was provided in the sleeping car on the Glasgow-London line in 1873. As far as aeroplanes were concerned, the first to be fitted with a lavatory was a giant Russian passenger plane in 1913, though it is not thought to have had water for flushing. It was the equivalent of a bucket privy rather than a WC. The first regular aeroplane to have an actual WC installed was the Handley Page W8, introduced on the London-Paris route in 1919.

[2]

How to Build a Privy

The Specialist is a book that describes the work of a fictional American carpenter, Lem Putt, who specialised in building privies. Written by Charles Sale, it is illustrated by the wonderfully named Frank Kermode. It has been in continuous publication in the UK since it first appeared in 1930.

It proves interesting to compare the advice he gives, originally aimed at an American audience, with the construction of privies in Derbyshire. The first privy Lem builds is a three-holer, made for an average family of eight. However, Lem is soon consulted by the purchaser who complains that his farmworkers are spending too much time in the privy. Lem checks and realises that he has made the seats far too comfortable. He saws the holes square – with hard edges – and the privy visiting time is immediately cut from 40 minutes to less than four!

The maliciously cruel idea of cutting uncomfortable square holes in a privy seat is older than one might imagine. I was surprised to discover square-cut holes in some garderobe privies I visited in the 15th-century wing of Haddon Hall, near Bakewell, originally the home of the Vernon family and now the home of the Dukes of Rutland. Obviously, the original aristocratic owners did not want their servants spending more than a couple of minutes on a visit to the garderobe.

Among the advice Lem Putt gives on privy construction is:

(a) Don't locate the privy under an apple tree, as there is nothing as disconcerting as the sound of apples dropping on the privy roof.

(b) Build the privy near the woodpile. There are two reasons for this: firstly, anyone using the privy can bring back four or five

25

A single garderobe for the use of the steward at Haddon Hall. Note the square-cut hole.

logs from the pile, thus filling the woodbox without extra journeys. Secondly, some women are shy about people knowing they're visiting the privy. They can go out to the woodpile, and check if anyone is watching before going in.

(c) Dig the hole under the privy deep and wide. It is far better to have a little privy over a big hole than a big privy over a small hole. Otherwise whenever you're in the privy, you're aware that you're soon going to need to relocate the building.

(d) Use beams in the floor rather than joists. Beams last longer, and if you have a gang of hard-drinking men visiting the privy together, singing and messing about, then they are running the risk of falling through into the pit below.

(e) A lean-to roof has some advantages over a pitch roof, since there are fewer corners for wasps to build a nest, and there's nothing worse than wasps buzzing round you while you're sitting on the privy. A lean-to roof also allows for a higher door.

A lean-to privy at Church Farm, Alsop-en-le-Dale.

Don Simmonds outside his privy at Bradley. The door was only five feet in height!

(f) Always have a nail from which to hang a mail order catalogue. This provides both reading matter, and the necessary paper for wiping purposes. Try to avoid those catalogues whose pages are made of hard shiny paper.

(g) A metal hook and eye fastener on the door is more reassuring than a piece of string, because sooner or later string wears out.

(h) Windows in a privy are possible but they are not a good idea, since anyone who finds the door fastened is tempted to look in through the window to see who's inside. This can disturb your privacy.

(i) Ventilation holes are useful. (Lem Putt offered star or crescent shaped holes, but was willing to carve entwining hearts for newly-wed couples.)

(j) Never use knotty wood for the walls. When a knot falls out,

This privy at Chinley had the recommended feature of facing away from the house, thus enabling the occupant to sit with the door open. Note the distance – uphill – from the house!

it never manages to be located at a good height for an occupant to look out, but frequently is just right for a passer-by to look in.

(k) Make the door so that it opens inwards. This enables you to sit in the privy with the door open, enjoying the sunshine, with the ability to kick it shut if you hear anyone approaching.

(l) Painting the outside of the structure red with clear white trimmings makes it easier to find the privy on a dark night.

(m) Anchor the privy down with a strong piece of 4 × 4 timber that runs from the top all the way down five feet into the ground. This makes it harder for devilish boys to tip the privy over on Halloween night, which can be unpleasant if it is occupied at the time.

Much of this advice is as true in Derbyshire as in rural America. Several Derbyshire ladies have told me how pleased they were that the dustbins were kept near the outside privy. 'I was very shy as a girl,' I was told, 'and I didn't like people to know I was going to the privy. It was very handy to pick up some piece of rubbish for the dustbin. Then when I got to the bin, I could check that no-one was watching and nip into the privy.' So item (b) has parallels locally, if we replace the notion of a wood-pile with that of a dustbin.

Item (c) is just as true in Derbyshire too. The pit under a privy had to be capacious, whether it was dug out once a month or twice a year. When the pit was replaced with a bucket, no Derbyshire dweller would be stupid enough to think of using a *small* bucket.

The nail for hanging paper from was just as necessary here, though the mail order catalogue was replaced by pieces cut from the daily or weekly newspaper. (Perhaps the increasing use of shiny paper in catalogues made it less suitable, for as one north Derbyshire native insisted on telling me, 'Hard shiny paper removes nothing; it merely rearranges.') Many older people recalled how, when they were children, it was their job on a Saturday morning to cut the newspaper into squares,

Mr and Mrs Nash and their privy at Basset Barn Farm, Dale Abbey. Note the ventilation holes in the brickwork!

A one-holer at Thorpe.

make a hole in one corner, and thread them onto string. One nice touch I heard was that the soft wrappers from oranges were always saved, and specially favoured visitors were allowed to use these.

Most privies I visited had no windows. Indeed there were few that had ventilation holes either. Perhaps the strong Derbyshire gales found their own way through the gaps above and below the doors, making stars and crescents unnecessary.

The inward opening door was standard. Many a Derbyshire man reflected Lem Putt's words, reminiscing that it was their common practice to sit with the door open, contemplating the view, while keeping one foot on the open door ready to kick it shut if they heard anyone approaching. It was noticeable that most privies had their door facing away from the house, making the open-door practice possible.

I found few privies painted in bright colours. Perhaps the native Derbyshire personality favoured letting the privy blend

in with its surroundings, at the expense of making it visible in the
dark. One lady who could have benefited from Lem's sound
advice told me that when she was a young woman, she was visiting her fiancé's parents for the first time. Being a 'townie', she
was not used to an outdoor privy, and when she set out to find it
one dark evening, she didn't think to take a torch or lantern with
her. After a hazardous trip of some fifty yards she did eventually
find the privy. Her journey back to the farmhouse was even
worse. She struggled through bushes and trees, across the
garden and waste ground. She eventually returned to the house
some 40 minutes after leaving it, dishevelled but relieved. 'And
do you know,' she told me, 'there they all sat talking. Not one
person had missed me, not even my fiancé!' It is greatly to the
lady's credit that she did in fact marry into this laid-back and
neglectful family.

Finally, the concept of anchoring the privy down with a long
wooden stake is completely foreign to Derbyshire. Mind you,

The privy at Dearleap Cottage, Handley, was roofed with heavy slabs.

some of the privies I visited had stone walls that were three feet thick, and roofs of heavy slates. No youngsters, no matter how much devilment was in them, would have much success in tipping over a Derbyshire privy at Halloween or on any other night.

This privy at Bradley was roofed with hexagonal tiles.

[3]

THOSE WERE THE DAYS

Richard Litchfield of Matlock informs me that when people painted the privy they used to put the bluebag used for washing clothes into the whitewash to give the walls a lovely pastel blue shade. He recently saw a house that had been pulled down in Tansley, and noticed that the two remaining walls of the privy still had that distinctive blue colour.

Mrs D. George of Chesterfield tells me that she remembers that during the 1940s the pub now called the Highwayman at Eastmoor, near Wadshelf, was then known as the New Inn. The landlady was a white haired, rosy-cheeked lady named Matilda Turner, who used to serve afternoon tea in the snug. Mrs George says that for 1/6d you got a boiled egg, brown bread, a scone and a pot of tea. The pub had a double privy situated in the courtyard at the back. The main problem with using these privies was that patrons had to cross a yard where there was a tethered black bull. Presumably, in order to face this bovine deterrent, you really had to be desperate to go!

Arthur Plumb grew up before the Great War in the village of Marlpool, near Heanor. At the far side of the backyard of his house in Prospect Row was a row of outbuildings, comprising a coalhouse and a privy with an ashpit. Some houses had a pigsty instead of a coalhouse. The privy had a candle holder fastened to the wall. Arthur remembers that there was always a canister of powerful smelling carbolic powder for sprinkling into the pan. In summer, one or two sticky fly-papers hung from the ceiling. Like many boys and girls at the time, it was Arthur's regular Saturday task to cut the newspapers into six-inch squares for use in the privy. The privy ashpits were emptied at regular intervals, always between 10 pm and 6 am. One man would shovel the contents through a small door, two feet square, into his mate's wheelbarrow. This was then wheeled down the entry to the nightsoil cart which was waiting on the road. The men used strong-smelling naptha lamps to illuminate their work, and the noise of the wheelbarrow's cast-iron wheel frequently woke the house's occupants. The nightsoil cart had a metal container with a tipping mechanism for emptying it, and a wooden seat on top for the workmen. At snap-time, the men would always sit on this seat to eat their sandwiches. Arthur remembers that one of the nightsoil men was called Caleb Riley. Caleb was a keen gardener and won lots of prizes at the local show for his celery. Arthur believes that this indicates that Caleb was in the habit of taking his work home with him; in other words, the prize celery was in part due to the use of nightsoil as fertiliser!

Marjorie Edge of Bolsover says that in the early 1930s her mother used to meet her and her sister out of Sunday School. They would walk $1\frac{1}{2}$ miles to visit her Aunty Flo who lived in a cottage nestled under the big wall surrounding Bolsover Castle. The two girls took a small basket with them, and their aunty would put some straw into it and three newly-laid eggs. Marjorie and her sister always wanted to visit the privy at Aunty Flo's, mainly because it was a two-holer and they could sit side by side, holding hands. They used to leave the door wide open, so that could enjoy the beautiful view of the castle.

Visiting her own outside privy was quite a performance in winter, Marjorie remembers. It involved putting on wellington boots, coat and hat, and sometimes carrying an umbrella for the long trek down the garden path. One day, Marjorie was sent to the shop for a loaf of bread, the shopkeeper wrapping the loaf in a sheet of tissue paper, as usual. On the way home, Marjorie decided to visit the privy, putting the bread next to her on the scrubbed wooden seat. That was where her mother found her, sitting on the privy, next to the loaf of bread. Marjorie remembers the incident vividly because her mother spanked her for her lack of hygiene.

I'm not sure what that fastidious lady would have made of the

John Williamson indicates the way to the old privy at Kennel Cottages, Calke.

story from Barbara Cooper's childhood in Somercotes. Barbara's friend Queenie sneaked a dish of sliced peaches out from her house, where her elder sister's wedding reception was taking place. The two girls took their stolen loot to the two-hole privy and sat there, happily eating the slices with their fingers. 'Thinking back,' says Barbara, 'those peaches were delicious.' Barbara also tells me that the outside privy was a favourite haunt of her brother Colin, in the days when he first started secret smoking. When her mother used to shout in to him, asking if he were smoking, Colin used to answer 'No!' but the cigarette smoke floating under and over the privy door gave the lie to his denials. Perhaps that privy was more pleasant than some, because it had an old-fashioned white rose tree growing just outside and Barbara can still remember the wonderful smell of the perfume from its roses. There was the odd snag, however, in the form of the free range hens that had the run of the garden. 'It was quite a shock,' says Barbara, 'to be sitting doing what comes naturally, when a squawk from a roosting fowl would scare you to death!'

A lady from Kirk Hallam told me that sixty years ago she lived in a terraced house there, with an open yard at the back. In the yard were five WCs and five coalhouses. She felt that she was very fortunate as there was one privy to each house, whereas her friend further along the road had only three WCs to five houses.

Ken Williams of Newbold, near Chesterfield, also grew up in a terraced house, in his case one of those built by the railway company in the mid-19th century to house its employees who worked in the engine sheds at Hasland. He remembers two rows of terraced houses, ten houses in one row and twelve in the other, the two rows being separated by a footpath. To get to the privy, Ken had to go to the bottom of the garden, through the gate and across the road. There was one building, known as a midden, for every two houses. Each midden had two privies, each with its own door, but sharing an ashpit. There was a side opening to the pit, into which both families would put their

Three privies in a row was a common arrangement, like these at Pilsley.

household waste, because there were no dustbins. They always knew when one elderly neighbour was in her privy because she used to leave the door ajar so that she could see anything happening down the road. It was quite rare to see any traffic, though, as the road ended at the terrace, and none of the residents had a car. The only traffic she would see was the milkman making his deliveries.

Ken was another who says that he used to cut the newspapers into squares and thread them onto string to hang on a nail in the privy. People using the privy would often start to read the squares of newspaper, invariably finding an item of news they couldn't remember reading before. The snag with this was that the reader would reach the most interesting part, only to find that it had been cut off. A rapid search through the remaining squares would, more often than not, prove that the piece needed to complete the reading was missing. What frustration!

Ralph Flintoff was born in Langley Mill, near Heanor, before the Great War. He became a builder and, during the 1930s, he was involved in converting a whole village of 400 houses from earth privies to flushing WCs, usually installing them in the coal-houses attached to the houses. Once, when fitting the wooden supports that were going to hold the cistern in a new WC, he was taken to task by an angry neighbour. Apparently, his hammering had caused the pots to fall off the kitchen wall next door. 'I hadn't realised that the walls were only $4\frac{1}{2}$ inches thick,' Ralph told me. 'I'd assumed they were twice that.'

Another fact that Ralph brought to my attention was the stick that was always kept in the old privies. This was about $2\frac{1}{2}$ feet long, and it was used to poke down any paper into the pit or the privy bucket, or to rearrange the pile of dung if it was beginning to assume a pyramid shape. As Ralph rightly pointed out, it was very important to remember which end of the stick was clean enough to hold, and which end was the dirty one. Ralph, and several other people who spoke to me subsequently, are strongly of the opinion that this is the origin of the phrase 'to get the dirty end of the stick', usually rendered in Derbyshire as 'to get the mucky end of the stick'.

[4]

GONGFERMORS AND OTHERS

Wherever there have been privies, there has been a need for someone to deal with the waste products. These men have been given various titles, official and unofficial. They were most commonly known as Nightsoil Men, or somewhat ironically as The Lavender Men or The Honey Dumpers. Evelyn Biggart of Kirk Langley and Ethel Young of Mickleover both remember them being called The Dilly Men, but to Barbara Cooper of Somercotes they were always The Bucket Bangers. In the Middle Ages they were known as gongfermors. The word gong meant a privy, from the Saxon word 'gang' meaning to go off, and fermor came from 'fey' meaning to cleanse.

The status afforded to these essential workers has varied through the ages. In Rome, the sewers were kept clean by convicts, who had no say in the matter of their occupation, let alone their position in society or their pay. The low status given to anyone working with sewers may be inferred from the fact that, during the reign of Tarquin I, a legion of Roman soldiers committed suicide when they were ordered to dig common sewers. They could not live with the knowledge that their status had plummeted from the height of being Roman legionaries to the very lowest.

However, in Medieval England the occupation of gongfermor was very highly rated. Raking out the cesspit at Newgate jail in 1281 required thirteen men working for five nights. For this work the men were paid handsomely, each earning 7d per night. This made them some of the highest paid men of their time. Moreover they could then sell the waste to farmers to use as fertiliser, thus increasing their income even more. In the 14th century, a John Lovegold, who had a monopoly to clean out the privies of London, was paid 2/6d a ton.

The work was not without its hazards; in 1326 a gongfermor called Richard the Raker fell through rotten boards into the cess-pit below, and drowned in the waste. On the other hand, being a gongfermor was once said to be a very healthy life! In the 17th century, it was widely believed that they were immune from the plague. They certainly got used to the smell, with working in it all the time. Somehow they filtered it out, while apparently retaining their sense of smell for other purposes. There is a recorded case of a gongfermor, who worked in the continuous pong of the cesspit, complaining to a fellow worker about the unpleasant smell of a candle that had recently been blown out.

The advantages of being a remover of waste were not, however, as apparent at the beginning of the 20th century. Desmond Holden of Bakewell told me a story of a situation his mother witnessed in 1910. A woman was nagging her son for not doing well at school. She went on and on, the boy growing more and more fed up. At the end of this long harangue, the woman came out with the classic question, 'Well, what **are** you going to do when you leave school?' The boy glowered and replied, 'I'll be a closet-emptier!' According to Mrs Holden, this answer caused great outrage. Desmond says that the modern equivalent might have been a boy telling his mother that he would become a drug-dealer or a pornographer. A closet-emptier was obviously the worst occupation the lad could think of.

Local poet Paul Fox has a poem on the subject of a man applying for the job of a lavatory attendant. The poem, called 'Why do you want this job?' contains the verses:

> My heart leaps when I see rows
> Of white enamel tiles,
> I dream of little cubicles
> That stretch for miles and miles.

Nightsoil man Edward Wilson, preparing to go collecting in 1911.
(Photo courtesy of Sylvia Starmer)

I'm fond of spotless basins
And plastic seats and bowls,
And making brass pipes sparkle
Has been one of my life's goals.

I want to help my fellow man —
To bring joy where's there's pain
And let him know that there's one place
Where he can call again.

I'll be the saviour of the sinks,
The doyen of the dunny,
For though I know that this job stinks
I'm desperate for the money.

Richard Litchfield recalls a story told to him by his mother who went to school in Ockbrook. The nightsoil cart had just reached the top of the hill on Green Lane when it was struck by the very first motor car in the village. The cart turned over and its contents flowed down the hill. Richard's mother and her schoolfriends had the unpleasant task of picking their way – no doubt with great care and with much horrified comment – through the sewage to get home. Richard is not sure of the date, but it must have happened in about 1919. He also recalls a similar accident on Victoria Avenue in Borrowash when a bus owned by Harry Oxley hit the nightsoil cart, sending the stuff everywhere!

Stewart Wayne of Marlpool had a great-uncle who was a nightsoil man, prior to 1925. He used to wear a hood and cape made from potato sacks. He was the limey-man, whose job was to come after the other men, strategically scattering lime over any spillages. All the privies had a metal bracket outside, and as the nightsoil men came to each one, they would put a naked flame torch into the bracket. Stewart's mother told him that the villagers could see the progress of the nightsoil men by the light display.

Stanley Hudson of Walton, near Chesterfield, says that his father had lived in a two room terraced house, where the nightsoil men had to carry the full container from the privy through the house, empty it into their cart, then return through the house with the empty can. Stanley says that although this must have been very unhygienic, his father lived a healthy life well into his eighties, as did several of his brothers and sisters. Stanley also told me the story of the local nightsoil man known as Mucky Dan, who used to enjoy his work except when it came to emptying the privies at the Workhouse, where the inmates were given too much 'jollop'. His main complaint was that there was nothing solid enough for him to stick his candle in, while he ate his bread and cheese!

Arthur Holmes of Little Eaton remembers living in Spondon as a child. He recalls the nightsoil men always coming at ten o'clock on a Sunday night. If it was summer, his mother would shout, 'Shut the windows, the nightsoil men are about.' The men used a metal open-topped cart drawn by a bay horse. When the cart was full, it was taken to a farm on Dale Road, to be emptied.

Mrs C. M. Wrigley of Kirk Hallam says that after her father died when she was eight she used to sleep with her mum. She remembers hearing the nightsoil cart and horse passing by late at night, and her mum telling her, 'That's the twelve o'clock horses!' This was in the 1930s, and it is interesting to note that the nightsoil men in this part of Derbyshire were still doing their collecting at night. By this time, most areas would have the collection done in the daytime, though the collectors were still called nightsoil men.

It is my view that the nightsoil men performed an essential task, and should have been granted their due status as invaluable members of the community in which they worked. People who looked down their noses – often literally – at them, or who denigrated them, were (a) being unfair and snobbish, and (b) running certain risks. Christine Liversuch remembers an incident from her childhood in Netherseal when a woman took a somewhat haughty tone with the man collecting the bucket from her privy. Christine says that the man did no more than lift the bucket onto his shoulder and take it towards the cart, 'accidentally' catching the edge of every sheet hanging on the woman's washing line.

Christine also recalls a wonderful story of a Netherseal lady walking down Main Street to catch the morning bus to Burton. The lady had taken great pains with her appearance. She was wearing a hat, a fur coat and high-heel shoes. Her make-up had been applied with great care. This elegant picture crumbled slightly when she saw Christine and bawled out, 'Ay up, Chris. 'As the shitcart bin yet?' The ironically euphemistic term The Honeycart had obviously not reached Netherseal!

In 1961, Mrs J. V. Brookes moved from a modern house with flushing WC to a cottage in Moneyash with a privy up the back yard. 'It was like stepping back in time!' she reminisces. Every Wednesday, the council lorry – nicknamed The Silver Bullet – used to come to empty the buckets. 'That was the day you kept all the doors and windows closed,' she says. On one occasion, next door's dog took a leap at the man carrying the full bucket on his shoulder to the lorry. The man was startled and the contents of the bucket poured down his back. 'He was none too pleased,' Mrs Brookes recalls. Dogs were obviously one more hazard of collecting nightsoil!

On the whole, nightsoil men were employed in Derbyshire towns and larger villages. For those people who lived in more remote places, it was necessary to dispose of the product of the privy for themselves. One man told me that his grandfather built his own house in Ockbrook in 1900. It had an outside privy with an extra large pit beneath, which was dug out once or twice a year. The waste was then buried in a hole in his orchard. When it was retrieved a year later, it looked like black treacle and was an excellent fertiliser.

A Spondon octogenarian recalls that his father used to empty their privy bucket on a Saturday or Sunday. After draining off the liquid, he would mix the remaining waste with sieved cinders from the fire and then take this mixture in a wheelbarrow to his allotment, which was about half a mile away. There he would leave it in piles for later use as fertiliser. 'Incidentally,' my informant states with pride, 'dad was always among the winners in the local flower, fruit and vegetable show.'

This pride in wonderful produce from gardens where the waste from privies was buried cropped up over and over again. John Wrigley, talking of his cottage in Kniveton, remembers growing prize gooseberry bushes of mammoth proportions.

Eighty years ago Patricia Benton was born at a pub called the Coach & Horses, on the Sheffield Road in Dronfield. A two-seater privy, which stood at the bottom of a very long garden, had a great deal of use as it served the patrons of the pub as well as members and supporters of the local football club which

45

played in the nearby field every Wednesday and Saturday. She and the other children were not allowed to use it, although the privy was spotlessly clean, being scrubbed out every day with steaming hot soda-water. Although the privy was emptied regularly by nightsoil men, Patricia's grandfather used to pipe off some of the contents for his compost bin, or 'swill bin' as he termed it. 'And', says Patricia, 'he had the best vegetables and flowers for miles around.' Although she thinks that the practice would be frowned upon today, she comments that they didn't suffer any ill effects.

Roger Webb's family moved to the village of Cutthorpe when he was two years old, to avoid the Sheffield blitz. The cottage they lived in had no gas, no electricity and no damp course. The privy, which was about 100 feet away at the end of the garden, backed onto that of their neighbour. Squeezed between the backs of the two privies was the pit, from which nightsoil was removed at infrequent intervals by a man – described by Roger as a 'malodorous individual' – with a horse and cart. Shortly after the Webbs moved in, the pit and the floors of the privies were concreted over, and a bucket system was installed. The contents of the buckets – newspaper and all – was thrown onto the garden and temporarily 'heeled in'. At bean planting time, Roger's father would dig a deep trench and fill it with the contents of the privies. As a result, his runner beans were superb, Roger recalls.

Pam Gee, of Kinder in the north-west of the county, says that locals would often grow a blackcurrant bush near the back of the privy, because the uric acid helped to grow big juicy fruits.

[5]

PRIVY HUMOUR

Barry Fearn tells me that his wife's aunty had a terrible fright while sitting on her privy. There she was, sitting and contemplating, when the cartmen arrived. They opened the back trapdoor and removed the bucket from beneath her before she knew what was happening. She heard the clatter, felt a sudden draught, and sat there quietly until the bucket was emptied and replaced. Whether the carters noticed anything amiss remains unrecorded. Perhaps, like aunty, it gave them a tale to tell and retell to their families over the years!

In some part of the county, the risk of catching someone in this embarrassing way was avoided as the collectors would sing as they worked, thus warning anyone using the privy that they were about. And their favourite song, according to Malcolm Tudor, was that old thirties melody, 'Tipitipitin'.

The grandparents of Anne Dutton used to live at a smallholding near Biggin-by-Hartington. Their outside privy was attached to the end of a shippon (or cowshed). They had a hen that would insist on laying her egg down inside the privy. She would jump down into one of the buckets and sometimes actually lay the egg on its contents. As Anne says, it hardly bears thinking about. Presumably the first task of the egg collector was to wash them all thoroughly. One well-loved family story is that on one occasion, grandad went out to the privy with his pipe and newspaper to sit and contemplate. He dropped his trousers, etc, and settled himself on the privy. Suddenly he became aware of a sharp commotion beneath him, and realised that the terrified hen was down below in the dark, trying to escape!

When I was giving a talk to the ladies of Doveridge WI in July 1997, I happened to mention that I was researching a book on Derbyshire privies. I related the above tale of the hen and the

47

Singer-songwriter Peter Glyde seeks inspiration outside his privy at Hart-shorne.

farmer, and heard one lady on the front row say to her neighbour, 'Well, it gives a whole new meaning to being henpecked!'

Two nightsoil men who used to work the Bakewell area were called Jock Kilbride and Charlie Chesterton. Richard Tomlinson once heard them being taken to task by a rather bossy council official about the length of time they were taking to empty the local earth closets. The official was carrying on at some length about whether they would be better to use a shovel or a fork to dig out the waste. Far from chastened, Jock Kilbride, who had a strong Irish accent and a short fuse, broke into the official's harangue with the very pertinent question, 'Whoever heard of anyone shovelling shit with a fork?' Apparently the official retreated.

According to a friend from Ilkeston, there were once two nightsoil men from that town – Bob and Alfie – who were doing their usual collecting. This was before the practice of taking away the full buckets and replacing them with clean ones. Bob and Alfie used to empty the buckets into their cart, and give their customers their own bucket back. Bob came back to the cart and was astounded to see Alfie rooting through the cartful of effluent. 'Alfie, what on earth are you doing?' he asked. 'Me coat's fell in,' Alfie explained. Bob pulled a disgusted face and advised Alfie to leave it where it was, since it was only an old jacket. 'Nay, lad, I'm not bothered about the jacket,' said Alfie, 'but me snap's in the pocket.'

One apocryphal story tells how, during the war, Sir Winston Churchill was sitting on the toilet when a light knock came on the door, followed by a whispered message that the Lord Privy Seal was waiting to see him. Churchill, annoyed at being interrupted in one of his more private moments, growled out in his inimitable style, 'Tell the Lord Privy Seal that I am sealed in my privy and I can only deal with one shit at a time.'

There are many words used to describe a chamber pot. It can be a jerry – and during the war I always assumed that it was spelled Gerry and somehow connected with the enemy. It can be a guzunder (because it guzunder the bed). However the most common term I remember from my childhood was the po (pronounced Poe). I remember when I was about 14, one Geography class coming to an uproarious standstill. There was a very clever girl in our class who always came top; the rest of us competed for the other placings. Although this girl was named Vicky, we all called her Flo since her middle name was Florence. The cause of the riot came when Mr Harrison, our Geography master, said during the course of a lesson on Italy that next week we would be looking at Florence on the Po. The class dissolved in howls, giggles and guffaws, and poor Flo suffered for months.

What is disposed of in the bucket of a privy is fairly obvious, but occasionally people have tried to extend the range. Tim, a farmer's son from Pilsley, decided that it would be a good way of getting rid of some waste engine oil from a tin he wanted to re-use. He poured it into the privy, thinking that it would get taken away with the rest of the waste. However, his father used the privy soon afterwards. Like many users, this man always

This two-holer at Lees Farm, Fenny Bentley, still has a bucket in place.

smoked while sitting on the loo. Smoking a Woodbine helped his reflective thoughts and, to be honest, it was also a darned good way of keeping off the flies and disguising the smell. His task completed, the farmer stood up and flicked his cigarette end into the bucket. Whoomph! The whole bucket burst into a mighty conflagration, scaring him witless, and singeing his flapping shirt-tail.

This reminded me of a story told to me by Richard Litchfield about the boyhood of his father, who came from Pinxton, a mining village near Alfreton. His privy had a wooden seat and lid that had become white over the years due to his mother frequently scrubbing it. Apparently she was a fanatic when it came to taking pride in its cleanliness. The boy used to mix his own gunpowder for fireworks and toy cannons, buying the chemicals at the local chemist's. He would lay the chemicals out in little piles on the privy lid, prior to mixing and packing them. One day when he was about thirteen, he was actually smoking a cigarette while he mixed the chemicals. Some hot ash fell from his cigarette and the whole lot blew up in his face, burning off his eyebrows and eyelashes. However, it was not his scorched face that troubled the boy. He had burned a huge black patch on the privy lid, and had to spend hours trying to scrub it off in order to hide it from his obsessionally privy-proud mum.

Another story from Richard concerned Stan, a man from Spondon who had been a butcher's boy in his youth. One windy morning he was cycling down Stoney Lane, now called Borrowash Road, with a basket full of meat to deliver. It was a lovely downhill ride for over a mile, so he had his feet up on the rests on the front forks. As Stan sped past a field where nightsoil had been tipped, the wind blew a sheet of newspaper which had been 'well immersed' over the hedge. It wrapped itself around Stan's head and fetched him off his bike. He then had to claw the dirty paper off his face, pick up the meat, brush it clean with his filthy hands, then continue down the hill to deliver it. As Richard says, it was a healthy life in those days!

In the late 19th century, one Derbyshire town was considering the building of a public Urinal. One alderman refused to vote for it, since he didn't know what the word meant, being more used to referring to bodily functions by more basic names. When the meaning of Urinal was explained to him in more homely terminology, he roared his approval and said enthusiastically that not only would he vote for the Urinal, but he would be happy to vote for an Arsenal as well.

Most of us view graffiti on lavatory walls with a mixture of amused disgust and tolerant disapproval. However, Derbyshire poet, Paul Fox, addresses his concern to a very different aspect, one that would-be writers neglect to their cost. In a poem, *Graffiti*, published in his wonderfully witty collection, *Midnight Jogger*, Paul writes:

I NEVER CEASE TO BE APPALLED
BY THOSE WHO WRITE ON TOILET WALLS —
DEPRAVITY AND FILTH AND LUST
ENGRAVED IN DARK CONVENIENT DUST —
FOR GOLDEN LADS AND WEIRDOS TOO
AS CHIMNEY-SWEEPERS USE THE LOO
AND HERE IT SEEMS THEY VENT THEIR SPLEEN
IN WRITINGS RACIST OR OBSCENE.
THEY RARELY SHOCK ME ANY MORE,
IT SEEMS I'VE READ THEM ALL BEFORE.
YET WHAT I FIND APPALS MY SIGHT
IS CASUAL LOSS OF COPYRIGHT.

[6]

A SOCIAL EVENT?

I have visited many two-hole privies throughout Derbyshire, and even one or two three-holers. My search for a rumoured four-holer at Brough House near Bradwell proved to be some years too late, but certainly four holers (and even six) live on in people's memory. Naturally, the existence of multi-hole privies led me to assume that people would visit the privy with a friend or two, a communal procedure. However, I was brought up short in my tracks by comments from a lady who, hearing my jocular observations about communal visits to the privy, told me sharply that this was not so. I had got it all wrong. The only reason for having a two-hole privy was that when one bucket

A two-hole privy at Blackbrook. Its owner – Mr Stirling – believes that the square hole in the wall level with the seat originally housed a sand/ash mechanism.

Dave Lakin inspects his two-holer at Dale Abbey.

became full, you moved over to the other one.

This made me think. Was this lady correct? Wouldn't it have been simpler to have the bucket emptied when it was getting full, rather than move over to the other seat? And how about those older privies where instead of a bucket there was simply a pit below? It would make no sense to change seat. I had to delve deeper!

In his book *All Quiet On The Western Front* Erich Maria Remarque writes of being sent as a young German soldier to the trenches in World War I. He tells how the young recruits were initially embarrassed at having to use the communal latrines, where up to twenty men would sit side by side as if on a train, under constant observation by their officers. Before long, however, the men regard the communal activity as a pleasure, as natural as eating or drinking together, and just as convivial. The privies, open to the blue sky and with views over the fields, become a place to smoke, to read, and to chat. The phrase 'latrine rumour' comes into use, reflecting the fact that the privy is the place to exchange news and gossip, the army equivalent of the street corner.

In the 1920s, Arthur Plumb of Marlpool remembers a large number of mature trees being felled on the Shipley Hall estate (now the American Adventure theme park), and a steam-powered sawmill being erected near Marlpool railway station. The privy provided for the use of the workmen was an open-fronted corrugated iron structure, fitted with a wooden pole placed two feet above a deep trench. Arthur was very impressed with the fact that this privy could seat ten men at a time!

But the communal privy is much older than these 20th-century memories; and far grander. In Timgad, a Roman city in North Africa, the large room set aside for such purposes had a fountain playing in the centre. No fewer than twenty-five stone seats were grouped around three sides of the room, each separated from its neighbour by a carved dolphin. This arrangement surely proves, for the Romans at least, that such activities were

considered a social activity to be performed in decorous surroundings. It was no different from eating or drinking; it was
something you did among friends.

Monks may have seen matters slightly differently though.
Sometimes their monastic privies, usually called rere-dorters or
necessaria, did give some privacy. These privies were parti-
tioned close on either side, so they could not see one another
when they were using them. Louis XIV, King of France, had
no such inhibitions however. He often held court and even
received foreign ambassadors while sitting on his commode. Of
course there were always those who took the notion of public
defecating too far. Lord Byron was barred from Long's Hotel in
Bond Street after an incident when, on a cold wet night, he
decided that the hallway was less inclement than the outside
yard. Still, the fact that he was barred did at least show that
this practice was dying out.

My friend Christine Liversuch grew up in the South Derbyshire village of Netherseal. Her house had a two-seater privy
that was joined to her neighbour's one-seater, separated by an
internal wall that reached almost to the roof. Christine recalls
that when her cousin came to visit, the two girls would often
visit the privy together. 'We were in our teens,' Christine says,
'and we would sit there for ages, talking girl talk, and exchange
confidences.' She was somewhat taken aback many years later to
be told by the boy who had grown up next door that he had often
sat in his own family privy – the one-seater – listening to the private all-female conversations of Christine and her cousin.

Roger Webb of Holmesfield was more inhibited. He says that
although he knew of double-seater privies, he never used one,
adding 'We were rather coy in the 1940s.' This is quite surprising
really, as he would only have been about seven by 1945. Roger
appears to have been in a minority, as other youngsters seemed
to have enjoyed the company.

Anne Dutton remembers being a child at a farm near Tissing-
ton, where water toilets were installed in 1962–63. Prior to that,

they used a brick-built two-holer privy. She recalls happily chatting away to her two cousins who were staying at the farm, as they sat there side by side. She says that this privy still exists, but is now rather dilapidated.

Going to the privy in company could have its drawbacks, though. Richard Tomlinson tells me that there used to be a trough privy at Ladybower. Here a number of visitors could sit side by side over a long, sloping channel, with water flowing along. Miscreants had a favourite trick of going to the upper hole, lighting a crumpled sheet of newspaper and sending it floating down the trough. To the delight of the perpetrators, the screams of people could be heard as the burning paper flowed beneath them.

John Wrigley used to live at Kniveton, near Ashbourne, in the 1930s. He well remembers going off exploring with a couple of female friends in the grounds of a mansion at Ashbourne Green. In the corner of the densely wooded grounds they discovered an old disused multi-privy over a stream. John, who would have been about eight at the time, says that he and his accomplices crawled underneath to gaze up goggle-eyed at the row of holes, imagining what it must have looked like when they were occupied. John could not recall the name of the house, but he thought it was occupied by a man named Mr Shwarby. After some detective work, my Kniveton friend Jean Moorley managed to work out from John's description that it must have been a house called The Grove. She had also heard from a former gardener there that the privy over the stream might still be there. I began to imagine what a wonderful photograph this would make. I contacted the owner of the Grove, Mr J. C. Ogle, who now lives in Brassington, but alas I found out that the privy over the stream finally blew down in the strong winds of 1987.

I never did track down a four-holer privy, though I did speak to people who can remember visiting such an establishment. I did, however, visit Harley Grange, a large farmhouse near Earl Sterndale. There I was delighted to discover a three-holer. This

A wonderful three-hole privy at Harley Grange, Earl Sterndale.

was a genuine three-holer, all the holes being of adult size, rather than a two-and-a-half hole privy which served two adults and a child.

My researches have led me to conclude that the lady who told me that people never used multi-hole privies in company must have been mistaken. While there may have been a few privy users too shy or too refined to do so, many Derbyshire residents have clear memories of making communal and convivial visits to the privy with a friend or two.

[7]

RURAL REMINISCENCES

I was at a friend's house in the summer of 1987, enjoying a barbecue in her garden. The friend was a teacher colleague, and this
annual barbecue was her way of celebrating the end of the school
summer term. I sat chatting to her father – a country builder
with a dry sense of humour and a knack of putting his finger on
the nub of any subject. As he put down his barbecued chicken
leg, and trudged off into the house to use the toilet, he turned
and looked at me. 'You know, son, it's all bloody back to front
these days. When I were a lad, we used to eat in the house and
crap up the garden!'

Mrs Mason of Ashbourne recalls a visit to Bamford Dams in

A row of derelict privies situated behind cottages in Buxton Road, Ashbourne.

1958, together with two friends. They found some tea rooms and enjoyed ham and eggs, bread and butter, with a pot of tea . . . and all for half a crown. After the meal, she asked the proprietor of the tea rooms if there was a toilet and was told to go outside and turn left. The three ladies set out like three jungle explorers, fighting their way through nettles that were three feet high. When they eventually reached the building they were amazed to find an old three-holer privy. 'We were laughing that much, and that stung by the nettles, that not one of us could manage to go when it came to it!' she tells me.

George Bardill used to empty the privies at Denby School, using a wheelbarrow to transport the product, before tipping it in the brook. As this was a voluntary task, undertaken one evening each week, his family was none too pleased to find him described in the school log book as a 'scavenger'. I sympathised with them; after all, a scavenger was someone who picked over waste tips for what he could use, or an animal that ate the leavings of another animal's catch. Or was it? When I consulted the *Shorter Oxford Dictionary*, I found among the more well-known definitions that scavengers could also be children employed in a spinning mill to collect loose cotton lying about the floor or machinery, men who removed the carbon deposits from the cylinders of an internal combustion engine, or anyone who removed discarded things. In India, it was the usual term used of the men who removed lavatorial waste. Perhaps the head teacher who wrote up the school log book at Denby had lived in India. I'm now sure that the description was not meant to be offensive.

Mrs G. Bussell has lived in six houses with privies. The first was in Staffordshire, but in 1930 she moved to the Derbyshire village of Kniveton to live in a small cottage in a field. There was no path to the stone-built privy, and no lights in the windowless building. A torch was necessary to go back and forth. The closet had a wooden seat, hinged to lift up so that her father could get the bucket out to go and bury its contents. In

1935 she moved to a semi-detached house at Ireton Wood. There the privy was brick-built, but again it had no window or light. However, things were more civilised here as there was a path running the thirty yards from the house to the privy. In 1945, when she moved to a house attached to farm buildings in Ashley Hay, it was a return to a situation where there was no path to the privy. As at Kniveton, the privy seat lifted for the removal of the bucket. Two years later, she was off to Idridgehay to live in a converted Victorian railway carriage. Here the bucket loo was in a wooden outbuilding attached to the carriage. One advantage here, at least from father's point of view, was that the bucket was emptied once a week by the Council night-soil men. Although she moved to a home with a flush toilet in 1950, Mrs Bussell returned to her roots in 1976–77, when she used a temporary chemical toilet situated in a cowshed while her cottage was being converted. As there was no door to the loo, this posed some difficulties when there were workmen on

Peter Downing was using his bucket privy until April 1997.

the site. As in her childhood, the contents of this bucket were buried in the cottage garden.

Peter Downing, who lives in a village in the Manifold valley on the Derbyshire/Staffordshire border, was using an outdoor privy regularly until the spring of 1997. The privy man used to come and empty the bucket every week. Once the man saw a dead badger near Peter's home, and enquired if he were going to keep the skin. Before Peter could answer, the bucket man had offered him the 'run-off' from the buckets to cure the skin in. Apparently, urine was used at one time in the curing of animal skins, despite the smell that lingered. So if your sheepskin coat smells when it gets wet . . .

Peter also recalls the winter when the village was cut off by snow drifts. They received information that a helicopter was

This is a photograph of Kinder Head Farm, now submerged beneath the water of Kinder Reservoir. The farm's privies are in the centre of the picture. (Photo courtesy of Pam Gee)

going to fly low over the farms and isolated cottages to see if anyone was in urgent need of supplies. Peter saw his neighbour Arthur out waiting for the helicopter, but when it didn't arrive, Arthur went into his privy. No sooner had he settled down than the helicopter swooped over. Arthur rushed out with his trousers round his ankles and his shirt-tail flapping, only to find the helicopter had gone. Disconsolately, he returned to the privy. Later that morning, Peter had a word with Arthur who was still grumbling about missing the helicopter, and asked him why he so badly wanted to flag it down. Was he perhaps in desperate need of something. 'Well,' said Arthur after a moment's consideration, 'I could do with a loaf.' Peter says he found it hard to imagine the pilot's expression if he'd been waved down, only to be asked to supply a small unsliced brown loaf.

A Derby lady also remembers snow drifts from her childhood. In the dreadful winter of 1947, her father had to cut out channels from the house to the privy. Jean says that the six foot high banks of snow loomed over her as she made the trip to the privy. That path to the privy was extremely important, and was always the first to be dug after heavy snow.

[8]

CASTLES, COTTAGES AND A DROVERS' ALEHOUSE

During my researches into the privies of Derbyshire, I was very fortunate to be able to visit some of the county's grander houses. Trips to Wingfield Manor and Bolsover Castle, both owned by English Heritage, proved particularly interesting. Wingfield Manor, near Alfreton, was built in the mid-15th century by Ralph, Lord Cromwell, though he was adding to an existing 12th-century castle. I was specially drawn to the High Tower, which once housed a very large communal latrine on the ground floor. This latrine was entered from the courtyard, and was thus available from all parts of the manor, not just the chambers above. There is some evidence that the privy had a wooden bench providing six seats. The waste would fall into the basement below, which had a pair of drains discharging onto the western slope of a hill. Rainwater from the roof of the tower was channelled into the basement via a 'chimney' in the thickness of the wall, and flushed the sewage out. However, this part of Wingfield Manor is now a picturesque ruin.

Bolsover Castle is a mansion built by the Cavendish family in the early 17th century, on the site of an earlier castle, and overlooks the town of Bolsover. It boasts a famous indoor riding school, but my interest was focused elsewhere. I had heard that, in one of the two lodges by the steps up to the 'Little Castle', there was an actual privy. I unlocked the door with high expectations but was disappointed to find that vandals had been there. The bench for the two-hole privy was leaning against the wall, its supports broken. A flagstone covered the hole where the privy once stood. From here I went into the Little Castle itself. This is situated on the highest part of the site, and on every floor the chambers have a door leading to a corner privy. What surprised

The High Tower at Wingfield Manor once housed a communal privy.

Haddon Hall.

me was that there were no holes in the floors here; every one of these privies – or 'stool closets' – would have had a bucket that had to be emptied on a regular basis by the servants.

My visit to Haddon Hall was even more rewarding. In addition to the square-cut holes in the two-seater garderobe, the indoor privy for the use of officials, and the single-hole privy that was probably for the use of the steward, another interesting feature was that one of the seats had a cover with a primitive lock. The key to the executive loo is a much older concept than I had realised!

Underneath the three privies was a large chamber. As at Wingfield Manor, a system of gutters channelled water into this chamber, flushing its contents out through an opening at the foot of the wall, and down a slope towards the nearby river. This practice was very common. Most castles had garderobes that emptied into a river or a moat. In course of time, the moats became so polluted that no attacker would dare to swim or

The entrance to the double privy at Haddon Hall.

wade through them! The Romans – much admired for their system of drains – simply sent the sewage down the steep hill-sides into the polluted river Tiber. They were more careful with urine, however. The Emperor Vespasian had street urinals con-structed, and sold the collected urine to the dyers and weavers for use in the workshops. Incidentally, street urinals in Paris are still sometimes called vespasiennes.

Enough of Rome and Paris. Let's return to Derbyshire.

In the town of Bakewell, two miles north of Haddon Hall, I visited the aptly named Old House Museum. Originally con-structed during the reign of Henry VIII and extended during the 17th century, the building is one of the oldest surviving domestic houses in the Peak District. It has had a chequered career. It was built by Ralph Gell, a wealthy lawyer, in 1534 and remained in the hands of the Gell family until 1798, when it was bought by Sir Richard Arkwright. He converted it into five small tenements for workers at his cotton mill. The building deteriorated over the next century and a half, and was con-demned as unfit for human habitation in 1954. Fortunately, it was saved from being demolished by members of Bakewell & District Historical Society, who bought the house and now run it as a museum.

In one of the bedrooms at Old House, the members of the His-torical Society found the original garderobe which had been blocked off and plastered over. This has now been opened up and its seat replaced. The garderobe lies between the house's two main fireplaces, which would be unthinkable today, because of the threat to hygiene. However the juxtaposition of fireplace and garderobe is not unique, and seems to be deliberate. One explanation, according to Dr Trevor Brighton who showed me round the house, is that the heat from the fires may have has-tened decomposition of the nightsoil. A side effect would have been that the garderobe would have been a pleasantly warm place to visit. The waste accumulated in the chamber beneath the garderobe, decomposing in the warmth, until it was sho-

Old House in Bakewell has an indoor garderobe.

Outside privies at Old House, Bakewell.

velled out. A sliding stone at the base of the outside wall gave access to the men who had this vital, if smelly, task.

The garderobe had been blocked off at the time that Arkwright was turning the house into workers' dwellings. To serve as its replacement, outside privies were built at the back of the house. Thus, Old House Museum today has both an indoor privy (garderobe) and a row of outdoor privies, enough to satisfy the keenest student of privy history.

Another residence I visited was Woodseats Hall, at Barlow, the home of Mr and Mrs Milward. The Hall itself dates from the 14th century; one family – the Mowers – owned it from that period until the 1960s. During the 17th and 18th centuries, various alterations and improvements were made to the Hall, and Rosemary Milward's researches have led her to date the privy as late 1600s or early 1700s. It was certainly in use until the 1960s. I am embarrassed to admit that I did ask the crass question as to whether Woodseats Hall took its name from its privy!

A substantial stone outbuilding, divided into two, houses this privy. The front compartment contains the wooden seat, which is a two-holer with a hinged wooden cover. In one wall is a recess that must have once held a candle or a lantern. The second compartment is about the same size as the first, and has an opening about 50 cm square, into the chamber below the privy seat. This back compartment has its own door so that ashes could be thrown in, and a window hole in the wall so that workmen could shovel out the waste, dropping it into a cart beneath. The waste was then used as fertiliser on the fields, as evidenced from an entry in the farm accounts which reads: 'Laid on the Horsecroft five loads of ashes and the privy dung.' However, the farm did not rely on the waste from the Hall. An entry of 1818 records the delivery of 'Four loads of rotten dung from Sheffield and 25 loads of rotten dung from Chesterfield.'

Another interesting two-seater privy I visited was at Younds

This detached privy at Boyleston is built of hand-made bricks. On the door is carved: WH 1811.

This little building at Blackbrook had a privy facing one way and a pigsty facing the other!

Cottage Farm, Boyleston. This was in a well-maintained detached building, built of hand-made bricks. The door was the original one, and bore a carved inscription: WH 1811. The present owner, John Parker, remembers being rather impressed when he took over the farm to find that the newspaper in the privy was in fact the *Financial Times*!

I also visited an old house at Blackbrook, a small hamlet near Chapel-en-le-Frith. The house, a former inn, stands on an old drovers' road, used by drovers travelling from Chester to York. 'Actually,' its owner told me, 'it would have been less of an inn, more of a common alehouse for the use of the drovers.' This too had a two-holer privy. The interesting fact here was that the privy shared a building with a pigsty. The privy faced the garden of the house, but the sty faced the other way. One unanswerable question that occurred to me was whether the drovers using the privy complained about the smell of the pigsty, or whether it was the poor pigs who suffered from the smell from next door! The contents of both the privy and the pigsty drained down a slope towards the local brook. It is perhaps not surprising that the area was called Blackbrook!

Some may find it shocking that those wonderful sparkling Derbyshire streams were used for dumping sewage. Castles and cottages alike were liable to dispose of their waste into a convenient stream or river. The water took it away, and that was all that mattered. What happened to it then was of little concern.

One place where the product of the privy fell directly into water was at Arkwright's Flour Mill in Cromford. I had been searching in vain for a privy built over a stream, and had virtually given up hope of finding one, when I had a phone call from Steve Pepper, a baker who works in the Cromford area. 'I hear you're looking for a privy over a stream,' he said. 'I know where there is one. It means a bit of a scramble down a wall, but we can easily get down to photograph it.' Of course I was delighted and went with Steve to the location. The wall he mentioned turned out to have a 15 foot drop on the other side, but two workmen from the Arkwright Society provided a ladder for me – Steve didn't really need it, as Derbyshire men seem to be born with the genes of mountain goats! However, the descent was achieved. The privy was a one-holer, and the waste from it fell directly into the millrace ten feet below. The users of this privy would have been very aware of the draught that must have howled up through the hole; it was obviously not a place to stay for a smoke and a read of the newspaper. There would have been no problem with privy smells, though.

At Handley, near Clay Cross, there is an interesting Grade II listed stone building known as Dearleap Cottage. It was built in 1790 as a school for 'poor children from North Wingfield'. It later became four cottages but its new owners, Mr and Mrs Cole, are restoring it to one building again. Here I found a sturdy two-seater privy, stone built and roofed with stone slabs.

Some of the privies I visited were in a dilapidated state, often

73

Privy at Arkwright's Flour Mill, Cromford. The waste fell directly into the
millrace below.

Dearleap Cottage, Handley, was built in 1790 as a school for poor children from North Wingfield.

This two-holer at Dearleap Cottage once served the needs of children living at the school.

This privy is part of a neat, tidy garden in Tunstead Milton – and now houses the barbecue equipment.

situated in a thicket of trees and bushes that involved hacking through, like the rescuer of Sleeping Beauty. Others were beautifully maintained and/or restored to their original condition. Many were being put to a different use, often serving as a garden store. One, at Tunstead Milton, housed the family barbecue. Another, at Chinley, was used for rearing baby chicks. At Twelvehouses, near Stanton Ironworks, the old privy was doorless and sheltering the modern wheelie-bin. Philip Mehew had removed the roof and upper half of the walls of his privy at Ashover. With the placing of a stone slab over the hole, he has now created a very original garden seat in a pleasant alcove, where he can sit, smoke and contemplate, three occupations that were probably followed when the privy was in use!

I also visited a plant nursery where the owner – Paul Lathrope – had used his old WC cistern, together with a garden roller, to form an unusual piece of sculpture!

Philip Mehew using the unusual garden seat formed from his old privy at Ash-over.

One thing to do with a disused WC cistern is to use it in a modern sculpture.

Not all the privies I visited were 'ancient monuments'. One was still used 'when we have a family garden party'. Another, at Larch Tree Farm in Hazelwood, was in regular use until October 1996; then there was the one at Grindon that was used until April 1997. The High Peak Borough Council, covering the Buxton area of the county, tell me that there are still six properties from which they 'collect the weekly contents of pail closets.'

[9]

BOYS BEHAVING BADLY – AND A MISCHIEVOUS MAID

As a young boy, Maurice Holmes of Ilkeston used to visit his cousins, who had a privy in their garden. It was actually one of a pair of privies, the other one belonging to the rather fierce woman who lived next door. This unfriendly neighbour used to be forever shouting at Maurice and his cousins, complaining that their playing was too noisy, and warning them to stay out of her privy. They took their revenge one summer by unfastening the goat that was tethered in the field nearby, and shutting it in the privy belonging to their 'enemy'. They then hid and waited until she came to go into her toilet. She opened the door, the enraged goat shot out and the boys were delighted with her resulting shrieks. Their sense of victory was so complete, it even made the good hiding that inevitably followed seem a merely temporary consequence.

Another childhood prank was recalled by an elegant white-haired lady who gave me a cup of tea in her best china tea service. This lady – who seemed so refined and well-spoken that I could hardly believe what she was telling me – recalled her childhood. Speaking in the best Queen's English, she told me that as a child she lived near to a row of three privies. When she and her female friends (fiends?) saw anyone go into one of the privies, they would wait for a moment, then pick themselves a number of very long-stemmed stinging nettles. Approaching on tiptoe, they would open the little door at the back of the privy, then thrust the nettles into the space between the bucket and the person sitting there. Ouch!

A very similar prank was played by Arthur Plumb. In 1924, when he was 11 years old, Arthur caught scarlet fever and went to stay for six weeks in the isolation hospital at Calladine House

A privy at the bottom of the garden, like here at Twelvehouses, near Stanton Ironworks, was the scene for many a childish prank.

in Loscoe. The ten boy inmates, led by a 14 year old called Jim Tebbett, crept to the back of the privy, carrying a long stick, opened the back trapdoor and disturbed the contemplations of the incumbent nurse.

Yet another perpetrator of this wicked practice was John Carrington of Inkersall. In the 1940s, John and his friends were playing street football in a place called Barber's Row, with goals chalked on a house wall. After a while, the owner of the house, a grumpy old man known as Bottles, emerged carrying a large kitchen knife. John and his fellow footballers fled, only to turn and see Bottles stick the knife into the pig's bladder they'd been using as a football. This meant war. John got his revenge a few days later, when Bottles was in his privy, by opening the rear trapdoor and thrashing about beneath the seated man with a branch from an elderberry bush. Although John got a slippering from his father, he still thinks it was worth it when he recalls the bull-like roaring emitted by Bottles when he was attacked from beneath in his privy.

Mrs J. V. Brookes tells me that her husband spent his childhood in Old Harpur. One favourite trick of the children there – though he swears he never did it – was to open the back door of the privy and throw a lighted newspaper under the sitter!

An even nastier trick was recalled by Arthur Siddal of Cromford. Some of the village lads would put drawing pins covered in dog dirt on the latches of the outside privies in the winter. The people who lived in the cottages would come down the garden path with a candle in a jam jar, fumble for the door and prick their thumbs as they went to press the latch down. What gave the village boys extra joy was that the injured party would then immediately put their thumb in their mouth and suck it. Disgusting!

One practical joke was played, not by children, but by the landlord of the Melbourne Arms, in Melbourne. Visitors to the ladies loo were confronted by a statue of Adam, complete with an enormous hinged figleaf. Any lady curious enough to lift the figleaf triggered a bell which rang in the pub bar. When the unsuspecting lady returned to her friends in the bar, she was invariably greeted with cheers and a chorus of 'You just had to look!'

A frequent trick was played by the older children in Melbourne, who used to congregate on the edge of the woods. The nearby field was one where the contents of the village privies was left to rot down. Quite why the children should choose that area to meet is one of those inexplicable questions that puzzle adults, but it obviously seemed a grand spot to the youngsters. Older children would take a long stick and poke it into the rotting dung, to get one end thoroughly soiled. When any younger children – or anyone very naive – turned up, the stick was always offered to them, in such a way that they took it by the dirty end. This hilarious joke was always known as Taking The Golden Rod.

[1 0]

THE ONWARD MARCH OF PROGRESS?

In his wonderful short story *The Contraption* the late Rhys Davies describes the power struggle between two powerful ladies: Sarah Crump, undisputed leader of nine elderly women living in the village almshouses, and her arch-foe, Mrs Hope-Cary. Although Mrs Hope-Cary has only lived in the village for ten years – or 'Five minutes!' as Sarah puts it – she has recently managed to get herself onto the committee overseeing the running of the almshouses and is determined to Make Improvements.

Mrs Hope-Cary has already forced 80-year-old Ida to open her permanently closed bedroom window, and has insisted that the nine reluctant women should cancel their Sunday news-papers and should wear matching frills on their heads. The resentment is already brewing and comes to a head when the women hear about the latest improvement – 'the contraption'. This is in fact a water closet. Now at the end of their tether, the women decide to make a final stand.

The contraption is installed at the back of the house shared by Ida Neate and Susie Eighteen, causing further annoyance when their garden is dug up to put in the pipework. Ida frightens the workmen by shouting at them, 'Donkey you can take to the well, but can't make him drink!'

The committee are nonplussed when the women refuse to use the latest Improvement, boycotting the new WC and continuing to use the old privy. Three weeks later, the Rector, very much under the thumb of Mrs Hope-Cary, calls a special meeting of the almshouses committee.

Sara Crump is the chosen spokesman for the women; a natural choice since it was she who had previously taken on the commit-tee to gain permission for the residents to wear their stockings in bed, and who had had the Sunday night supper of cold fish pie replaced by tinned salmon. However, those victories were in the days before the arrival of Mrs Hope-Cary. Sarah's task is now much harder.

Dressed in her best black satin, Sarah attends the meeting. The other women have showered her with advice, much of it contradictory: she is to be firm and resolute, she is to remain ladylike at all times. She is to remind the committee how Chrissie Inge had asked for gin the day before she died and was denied it.

At the meeting, held in the village hall, Sarah sits facing the line of committee members. She knows that she will have some on her side, particularly Colonel Cole with a twinkle in his eye, and old Sam Lime who can remember her when she was a young village May Queen. Mrs Hope-Cary sits stony-faced, however, and the other ladies of the committee seem to be in awe of her.

Eventually the diffident Rector asks Sarah if she can give some explanation about the women scorning to use the new installation. Mrs Hope-Cary interrupts sharply, accusing Sarah Crump of being the ringleader of the women who are being obstinate, wicked and foolish. Sarah inclines her head in a practised regal bow, and thanks Mrs Hope-Cary for speaking plainly, before coming out with an explanation that leaves the whole committee speechless. Addressing herself to the Rector, she states, 'Well, sir, it's because me and the ladies can't bring ourselves to sit over water.'

When Mrs Hope-Cary recovers enough to threaten to have the old privy removed, Sarah remains adamant. Other members of the committee try coaxing, but Sarah is as immune to that as she is to threats. The women will not use the new contraption. When eventually one brave member asks what the ladies will do when the old privy is taken down, Sarah replies that they would have to 'use the hedges betwix the fields.'

When Sarah leaves the meeting, she knows in her heart that she has won: the 'old place' will not be dismantled. When she reports back to her friends she tells them that, in her opinion,

Mrs Hope-Cary will not be able to live with her defeat and will resign from the committee. Sarah is proved right; Mrs Hope-Cary decides to take up politics instead, and is rumoured to be planning to be the Tory candidate in the next election. Sarah and the residents of the almshouses have triumphed and the enemy has been routed.

In later years, all visitors to the almshouses are told the story of the famous struggle between Sarah Crump and Mrs Hope-Cary and may even be shown the now derelict 'new contraption'. It is still unused. No-one has ever had to sit over water!

Some Derbyshire residents, like those in Rhys Davies's story, look back with nostalgia to the days of the privy. One lady told me that her father thought the idea of having a lavatory inside the house was (a) disgusting and (b) eccentric, and unlikely to catch on. He wanted to remain true to the outside privy, but others were far less keen.

Shirley Williamson, from Whaley Bridge, lived in a cottage with an outside privy until she was four, before moving to a house with indoor facilities. Even at that age, she remembers thinking how wonderful it was to have a warm indoor loo. However, when she was 25 she moved to a little cottage and it was back to the outside visits again. One thing she didn't like was that if you had run out of paper or were renewing it all the neighbours knew where you were going as you crossed the yard, paper in hand. Shirley used to hide it up her jumper to avoid this embarrassment. She says that at least in your own home no-one knows when you go to the loo. Shirley, who is definitely of the 'march of progress' faction, has put her feeling into verse:

> We had an outside toilet
> Up the steps, across the yard.
> Freezing cold and dark inside
> And ooh – the seat was hard!

A pair of outside WCs at Whaley Bridge. (Photo courtesy of Shirley Williamson)

> As I'd climb up and sit there,
> Feet swinging off the ground.
> My eyes accustomed to the dark,
> The spiders would come down!
>
> I'd blow on them to make them run,
> Up to their webs they'd go.
> I never stayed in there too long,
> Especially not in snow!!

You were far more likely to meet large spiders in an outside privy than in a clean indoor WC. You could, like Shirley Williamson, blow on them or you could offer them tribute to keep them occupied. Mrs Rigley recalls visiting her grandmother's house in Anchor Row, Ilkeston. She used to catch flies and put them into the huge spiders' webs that hung in the privy.

Arthur Holmes was even more cruel, pulling the wings off the flies to watch them crawl around the seat before flicking them into the privy to drown. Ah yes, you certainly had to make your own fun in those days!

Another hazard of the outside privy was the presence of mice. Mrs Brookes of Bamford says that she would always make a lot of noise and give the privy door a good kick before entering, to give the mice time to run away and hide.

Roger Webb, who as a boy lived at Cutthorpe in the 1940s, says that their privy backed onto that of his neighbour, Mr Brown, a man of regular habits. He would whistle his way to the privy at 7.05 each morning with his *Daily Mail* under his arm, returning at 7.10 and catching the bus to Chesterfield at 7.20. Roger's father had a much more relaxed attitude. His visit to the privy was one of life's pleasures, one to be enjoyed at leisure. On a Sunday afternoon, he would amble up the garden in his carpet slippers, carrying a pint pot of tea, two slices of toast, the *News of the World*, his pipe and tobacco pouch, and a box of Swan Vestas. Whenever Roger asked his mother, 'Where's my dad?' she would reply, 'Where do you think!' If Roger went to investigate, he would discover a silent privy with a stream of tobacco smoke emerging through the heart-shaped ventilation hole in the door. Father's hour-long visits to the privy did not mean that no-one else could go, but anyone expressing a wish to use the facility would be met by a blistering and ferocious complaint from within, the general theme being that it was a poor how-do-you-do if a chap couldn't visit his privy in peace.

In the mid-1950s, the landlord converted the outside privies to water closets. This was not altogether a forward step, as far as Roger's family was concerned. They still had a candle on the ledge, but now it had to be joined by a hurricane lamp which burned all winter to stop the pipes from freezing up. The soft newspaper was replaced by shiny Izal toilet paper, again not an entirely unmixed blessing. Roger's father, who now had to pay

The advent of outside WCs brought the additional problem of the cistern and pipes freezing up in winter. (Photo courtesy of Shirley Williamson)

for garden manure to be delivered, thought that the installation of a water closet was a definitely retrograde step.

Marjorie Taylor lived at Lower House Farm, Quarnford, from 1962–73. When she first moved in they used an outside privy for six months while the house was being renovated. By Christmas, they had an indoors WC. Progress had triumphed over the old ways. But then the terrible 1962–63 blizzards and severe frosts came, and the new loo froze up. Marjorie and her family solved the problem by returning to the privy in the yard. I'm sure that Sarah Crump and the ladies of the almshouses would have approved.

On the surface it would appear that, whatever the pros and cons of the old privy, the new water closets did have the benefit of improved hygiene. But was that actually true? Valuable ammunition for the anti-WC brigade was provided by microbiologist Dr Chuck Gerba, who asserted that every time a WC is flushed, a cloud of invisible spray is released into the air. Dr Gerba calculated that this spray, which contains thousands of bacteria from the toilet bowl, settles over everything – and everyone – within six feet. Closing the toilet lid has only a temporary effect. The next person to lift it will receive the full 'benefit' of the delayed germ-laden aerosol spray. So, once again, the privy people may have some validity in their preference.

However, even the strongest supporters of the old privy have to admit that the one drawback of their preferred system was the smell. Several Derbyshire residents told me, 'The one thing that I remember from our privy was the terrible smell!' Local poet Malcolm Tudor put the danger of this ubiquitous and malodorous phenomenon into verse, part of which is quoted here:

There's a smell coming up from the garden.
I know what is causing the pong
For the door is ajar in the privy
And the nightsoil gang left it too long.
You can cover what's there with some paper,
Sprinkle some lime on the top,
Scrub hard on the seat with carbolic,
But the pong is so strong it won't stop.

If the wind is this way there's a problem
For a haze will drift up the back yard.
It kills all the flowers and the rhubarb
And starches the washing brick hard.
The paint on the house is all blistered,
Though the weeds seem to flourish and thrive,
But it must have got through to the pantry
For the mice are more dead than alive.

The baker and butcher stopped calling,
The postman refuses alike,
As his wheels are both prone to collapsing
For the fumes are corroding his bike.
The Co-op don't send any parcels,
The milkman's not been as of late.
It's said that the smell made his mind up
To sell up and then emigrate.

[11]

AND FINALLY . . .

This rhyme, which comes in the form of a limerick, was sent to me by an elderly gentleman from Glossop. I guess it refers to one of Derbyshire's two-holers!

> There was a young man name of Hyde
> Who fell in his privy and died,
> Then his twin brother
> Fell into another
> And now they're interred side by side.

───────────

The good friend who was the source of the quote that concluded the introduction to this book insists on one final word. 'At last it's official, David,' he says. 'You ARE a crap writer!'

A Privy By Any Other Name

A 'certain' place
Asterroom
Aunt Jane's
Biffy
Bog
Boghouse
Bombay
Chamberlain pianos ('bucket lav')
Chamber of Commerce
Chuggie
Closet
Comfort station
Crapphouse
Crapping castle
Dike
Dinkum-dunnies
Doneks
Dubs
Duffs
Dunnekin
Dunnick
Dyke
Garden loo
Garderobe
Go and have a Jimmy Riddle
Go and have a Tom Tit
Going to pick the daisies
Going to see a man about a dog
Going to stack the tools
Going to the George
Going to the groves
Going where the wind is always blowing
Gong
Gong house
Heads
Here is are
Holy of holies
Honk
House of commons
House of office
Houses of parliament
Jakes
Jericho
Jerry-come-tumble
Karzi
Klondike
Larties
Latrine
Lavatory
Little house
Midden
Necessarium
Netty
Out the back
Petty
Place of easement
Place of repose

Place of retirement
Reading room
Round-the-back
Shit-hole
Shittush
Shooting gallery
Shunkie
Slash house
The backhouse
The boggy at the bottom
The bush
The dispensary
The dunny
The grot
The halting station Hoojy-boo (attributed to Dame Edith Evans)
The house where the emperor goes on foot
The hum
The jakers
The jampot
The japping
The John
The lats
The long drop
The opportunity
The ping-pong house
The proverbial
The Sammy
The shants
The shot-tower
The sociable
The tandem (a two-holer)
The thinking house

The throne room
The watteries
The wee house
The whajucallit
Three and more seaters
Thunder box
Two-seaters
Widdlehouse
Windsor Castle
'Yer Tiz'

Especially for WCs:
Adam & Eve
Chain of events
Flushes and blushes
Going to inspect the plumbing
The penny house
The plumbing
The porcelain pony
The urinal
The water box
Umtag (Russian version of the WC)
Waterloo

The term 'privy' is an Early Middle English word which derives from the Latin 'privatus' meaning apart or secret.

ACKNOWLEDGEMENTS

I would like to thank Lewis Davies for allowing me to refer to the opinions of the wonderful characters in *The Contraption*, a story by his brother, the late Rhys Davies. My thanks too to Paul Fox for allowing me to quote poems from his books *Midnight Jogger* and *An Explosion and Something Red*. I would also like to express my thanks to John O'Brien, Comptroller of Haddon Hall, for letting me visit there with my camera, to English Heritage, for giving me similar permission to take photographs at Wingfield Hall and Bolsover Castle, and to Dr Trevor Brighton, chairman of Bakewell Historical Society, who conducted me round Old House Museum.

I would also like to put on record my gratitude to officers of Derbyshire County Council, Derbyshire Dales District Council, High Peak Borough Council, Erewash Borough Council, South Derbyshire District Council and Amber Valley Borough Council, who helped my researches in different ways.

My largest debt of gratitude is to the innumerable Derbyshire men and women who got in touch with me, after my appeal for information on Radio Derby and the local newspapers. They sent me their humorous and/or nostalgic reminiscences, and often invited me to come and take photographs of their privies. The people to whom I owe thanks include: Dennis Ashton, Patricia Benton, Evelyn Biggart, Mr & Mrs Bratt, Mrs M. F. Brindley, Mrs J. V. Brookes, Mrs G. Bussell, John Carrington, Sheila Cook, Barbara Cooper, Mrs J. K. Cole, Mr & Mrs Roy Collier, Mrs Copestake, Marjorie Davies, Peter Downing, Mrs Duffell, Anne Dutton, Marjorie Edge, Barry Fearn, Mick Finnikin, Ralph Flintoff, Julie Froggett, Derek Fox, Pam Gee, Mrs D. George, Barbara Hodgkinson, Desmond Holden, Arthur Holmes, Maurice Holmes, Mr Hoult, Stanley Hudson, Mrs

Michael Hurt, Dave Lakin, Richard Litchfield, Chris Liversuch, Mrs Mason, Mrs McLoughlan, Philip Mehew, Mrs Rosemary Milward, Alison Mitchell & John Williamson, Frank Money, Mr & Mrs P. Nash, Mr J. C. Ogle, John Parker, Steve Pepper, Arthur Plumb, John Randles, June Reeves, Mrs C. M. Rigley, Iris Shepherd, Don Simmonds, Mrs J. Smith, Mrs Starmer, Mr Stirling, Marjorie Taylor, Jean Thornhill, Richard Tomlinson, Malcolm Tudor, Mrs Vesty, Stewart Wayne, Roger Webb, Mrs Weightman, Ken Williams, Shirley Williamson, John Charles Wrigley, Mrs C. M. Wrigley and Ethel Young.